Some Suffolk Squit

By Adie Copping

1

ISBN 978-0-9562243-8-5

Published by Polstead Press
5A The Maltings, Stowupland Road, Stowmarket,
Suffolk IP14 5AG

Tel: 01449 677500
Fax: 01449 770028
Email: info@ghyllhouse.co.uk

Acknowledgements.

Many thanks to my friends
Kim and Mark,
Vanessa and Bob,
Gary the yachtsman,
and Julian G.
for their comments and input.
And also my son Brad for his
guidance on the use of
the computer.

'I don't think I'll ever get the hang of it!'

Introduction

Welcome to Some Suffolk Squit!

Thank you for taking the time to read this introduction because it just might sway you into buying this book, if you haven't already.

If you're a visitor to Suffolk and want to decipher some of the Suffolk 'Lingo', then reading through this book should help you get your ear holes attuned to this very old and strange accent.

If you want to teach yourself to speak fluent Suffolk, then this book could possibly help you on your way, but you'll have to give yourself about ten years for the accent to roll off the tongue smoothly as there hasn't been a single actor on TV that can do it yet!

Or if you're already a Suff'cker born and bred, then this book just might open your eyes (and your ears) to something you take for granted everyday.

You will – hopefully after reading this book - become more aware of what you, your family and friends actually say - so much so, you'll be stunned I promise you!

And finally, if you just want a bit of daftness in your life with the Suffolk 'Lingo' thrown in for good measure, please read on. I do hope you enjoy it.

WARNING!

You may find this book difficult to read in places so please read the 'Helpful guide to this book' section first, as you may find yourself reading a sentence - or two - several times trying to make out what its saying - I don't want you getting all frustrated and giving yourself a headache now!

Guide to Using This Book

If like me, you've read these sort of books before, you'll know that it's not easy to read oddly worded sentences with a nice flow. You will often reach a word that will stop you in your tracks with a "What's that?" or "How do I pronounce that?" and that flow of reading something funny could easily fall apart - a bit like someone telling a joke and then ruining the punch line!

Now, with this book - hopefully - you will be able to gradually build up your repertoire of words and read the latter pages of this book with relative ease.

A good amount of the words are written normally because they are probably said quite normally, while some of the words you would expect to be spelt differently, because they're said differently, I've purposely left alone to avoid confusing you more than you need. Confused already…? Me too!

A general rule of thumb with the Suffolk accent is that we Suffolk folk very rarely pronounce the letter 'T' correctly. At the beginning of a word we do, but at the end or middle of a word, we don't! - Its there, but in a kind of silent mode. For example:- 'That don't matter', would be said like 'Tha' don' ma'er', you know what's being said but you won't hear clear cut 'Tee's'. As I said earlier, I would have to print the word 'matter' with the 't's' intact, otherwise you wouldn't know what it was. So, just remember, tall, toad, stone, stood and the like, use the 'T' at the beginning and everything else has the silent treatment.

The letter 'I' is very noticeable in Suffolk as it doesn't really exist as 'Eye', but more of an 'Oi' as in toy, eg. 'Oi went out on a broight noight'. Did you remember the silent 'Tee's?' - If you did you're dorn well! Sorry, meant 'doing well!'

'Ing' is something you won't find very often. Most words ending in 'ing' will generally be an 'en' or an 'un', it can vary; e.g. shoppun, diggun, washun, revven, tellen. 'Going' and 'doing' are slightly different and are usually said as 'gorn' and 'dorn' as in dawn.

There are words that use the 'ing', like, thing, sing, fling, tingle and sting, but there aren't that many.

The letter 'O' can be a tricky one as this can really be abused. It will get distorted in a variety of ways and will vary from town to town.

Some people will say the words 'road' and 'stones' as ruud and stuuns as in hood or stood - for some strange reason I might say these words correctly one day and not the next - perhaps it all depends on whom I'm talking to!

Go, to, so, throw, blow and all similar words can vary as I had said. Some people will pronounce 'go' as gew, others might say goo, gow or geow - I decided to go for gew and tew for this book!

'T' aitches get dropped in places too, not all the time as it depends on what is being said. 'That's alright then' can vary in a few ways. It could be 'ass alroight en' or 'thas alroight den'-peculiar or what?

Now for the difficult part. Us Suffolk folk are known for talking in a kind of shorthand way. Several words can be joined together almost forming one long word; e.g; 'I would like one of them'- 'Oi'd loike wunna'nem' or 'Have you got them?'- 'Hay y'gottum? It's no wonder we get a funny look and an 'I beg your pardon' to go with it!

On each proceeding page to the verses you're about to read, I have printed the Suffolk wordings you're about to encounter within the verses, so that you can be prepared for their meaning and to enable you to get a feel for the pronunciation, thus allowing you to read the whole thing with a nice constant flow - well that's the theory anyway!

To add some flavour to the verses, you'll have to imagine that an old farmer boy is reciting the verse to you, with the old 'ooh - arrhs', it will help, I assure you.

I must apologize here and now if I've offended any farmers out there who are not in the slightest way an 'ooh-arrh' type of person, but just remember, the English language was born here in Suffolk and whatever word is spoken in whatsoever form elsewhere around the country, it spread out from hear in Suffolk first and evolved outwards like ripples on a pond. The Suffolk voice has to be the most important of all to keep alive and must never be lost.

oi ... I

onnis ... on this

sunshoine ...sunshine

clewds ...clouds

injoyun ...enjoying

ponderun ... pondering

sew ...so

whoiy ...why

Oi lay onnis hill
                ponderun away,

injoyun the sunshoine
                onnis glorious day,

clewds are fluffy,
                tree's are not,

whoiy are me feet
                sew flippun hot?

oi wer … I was

uvver … other

boike … bike

hed … had

blew … blue

Oi wer on me boike
　　　　the uvver day

when oi saw meself
　　　　comin' the uvver way,

strange oi thought
　　　　where hed oi been?

Tha' boike is blew,
　　　　an' this one's green!

dew ... do

loike ... like

tew ... to

cloimb ... climb

thas ... that's

gittun ... getting

orn ... on

git ... get

h'grewn ... have grown

lorng ... long

gorn ... going

sew ... so

hew ... how

uts ... it's (pronounced as a quickly said ertz)

Oi dew loike
        tew cloimb a tree

tew git up there
        an' see wha' oi can see,

thas no trouble
        gittun orn up,

uts comin' dewn
        when oi git stuck.

Hew come me legs
        h'grewn sew short?

They wer lorng enough
        gorn up, oi thought!

ee … he

int … isn't

arf … half

whoile … while

ut … it

wivva … with a

boiy … boy

marnt …must not

dornnat … doing that

grut … great

nivver … never

ole … old

Oi've got meself a puppy dawg

 ee int arf alotta fun,

whoile oi be a trainun ut

 oi reward ut wivva bun,

"Boiy, yew marnt be a dornnat!"

Oi hear from me Dad,

"Tha' dawg'll git a grut ole thing

an' yew'll wish yew nivver 'ad!"

wennut … when it

geud …good (pronounced as in bird)

snew … snow

hoss … horse

moight … might

wanna … want to

slew … slow

gew … go

t'whairoiy … to where I

Cars a come
          an' cars a gew,

but int alotta geud
             wennut snew,

but moiy ole hoss
            tha' oi call Floss,

through the deep stuff
           she'll gew.

She moight be stubborn,
              she moight be slew,

but ut least oi git
             t'whairoiy wanna gew.

wassa ... was a

o'moine ... of mine

unna ... and a

nair ... there

innat ... in that

lissen ... listen

inna ... in a

huzzun ... (whizzing about)

yewwa ... you are a

slew dewn ... slow down

couz ... because (pronounced as in 'could')

hew ... who

toime ... time

new ... now

spind ... spend

nivver ... never

grut ... great

Oi wassa talkun tew a friend o'moine

hew nivver seem t'ave the toime,

a huzzun here unna huzzun nair,

'slew dewn!' oi said, 'an' sit innat chair.'

'New lissen boiy, yew gotta change yor way,

couz yewwa dorn tew much inna single day.'

'Be loike me!' oi said, 'A man wiv outta care,

an' spind more toime a sittin' dewn,

on yer arse, inna grut armchair!'

oi'll … I will

couz … because

uz … is

duzzy … (word used instead of dozey or dopey)

Rewses are red,

Violuts are blew,

oime not sew sure,

hew about yew?

Oi'll av tew change these glasses,

couz thing's are gittin' bad,

oi asked me Mum a question,

but wer talkun tew me Dad.

"Boiy, cant yew see proper?" he said

" Ya Ma uz over there!

Ask her t'git 'em scissors out

an' cut tha' duzzy hair!"

spoiders … spiders

avgot … have got

froiyun … frying

sumfun … something

izzut … is it

ouwn … own (pronounced as in brown)

winnay … when they

cannay … can they

floiyes … flies

oiyes … eyes

'undruds … hundreds

anuvva … another

George 'nd Reg.

"Ay Reg, dew yew reckon spoiders avgot non-stick feet

loike a froiyun pan or sumfun, couz hew izzut they don't

stick tew thar ouwn webs?...

Oi mean,winnay git stuck inna bath th'cant git out
cannay!"

"...An' anuvva thing, whoiy izzut tha' floiyes avgot
'undruds ov oiyes,
but cant see 'em spoiders webs?"

tractus … tractors

boy … by

grut … great

gettum … get them

dewn …down

trewth … truth

thattera … that are

ivry … every

uts … it's

Tractus are loiked
            boy all the boys,

be 'em real or
            be 'em toys,

them grut ole wheels
            thattera on the back,

will gettum through
            the muddiest track.

Up 'nd dewn the
            fields oi gew,

each 'nd ivry mornun …

Sorry!
 Hold ut roight there,

            oi gotta tell ya the trewth

   UTS FLIPPIN' BORIN'!

hew … how

cowmb … comb

ut … it

loike … like

o'moine … of mine

acrorst … acrossed

Hew dew yew cowmb ya hair?

Dew yew part ut tew the left,

dew yew part ut tew the roight

or don't yew really care.

Or are yew loike a mate o'moine

who does 'is really queer,

parted roight acrorst the middle,

from ear tew flippin' ear!

ruud … road (pronounced as in hood or stood)

crorssed … crossed

uvver … other

'it … hit

coont … couldn't

foind … find

bitta … bit of

arta … after

Oi crorssed the ruud the uvver day

an' gort 'it boiy a car…

Oi couldn't foind me bitta chalk arta tha'!

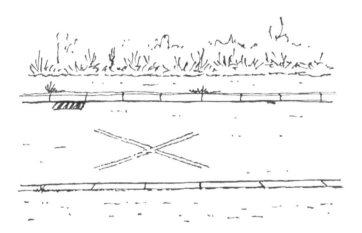

wuz … was

whews … who's

frinds … friends

chewun … chewing

floies … flies

catchun … catching

noight … night

huum … home (pronounced as in hood)

There wuz this bat
        tha' hadda ball,
whews frinds did come
        tew this grut big hall.

thay flew about
        the chimney tops,
chewun floies
        an' catchun moths.

Thay danced all noight
        an' hed such fun,
then flew back huum
        from whence thay come.

"EES GOTTA HEN'GEWVA...
HIS OLE HEADSA HUTTUN!"

gort … got

lorst … lost

atellin' … a telling

"Eeya, Reg' oi werra thinkun …

    If 'em ole moths loike broight lights sew much,

    whoiy don' thay come out inna daytoime?

Oi gort lorst
      the uvver day,

where oi wer
      oi couldn't say,

if oi knew
      where oi wer,

oi'd be ixplainun ut
      an' atellun yer!

onna … on a

gort … got

hed … head

loight … light   soight … sight

lorst … lost

soide … side

hoiy … high

toide … tide

hewle … whole

Oi stood onna cliff
   an' gotta whiff
   ov tha' lovely fresh sea air,

me hed gort sew loight
   oi lorst me soight
   an' hed tew sit inna chair.

" Tis good fer yew!"
   Said moiy good woife Sue,
"Ut'll help yew sleep fer sure!"

Had oi fell over the soide
   wiv out a hoiy toide,
   oi'd be a sleepun a hewle lot more!

When does a stream
              b'come a river,

when does a pond
              b'come a lake,

when does a sea
              b'come an ocean

or a bun b'come a cake?

Uts conker toime,

Oh what fun,

'slong as moiy opponunt

don't smash me fumb!

blackbud … blackbird

foight … fight

moight … might

hew … how

uts … it's

mewst … most

naow … no

A new day
        a new dawn,

there's a blackbud
        on me lawn.

He grabs a worm
        an' has a foight,

he pulls an' pulls
        wiv all his moight.

The worm foights back
        an' kills the bird,

hew can this be,
        uts mewst absurd.

Silly me,
        uts moiy mistake,

tha' int naow worm,
        ut wer a snake!

newtussed … noticed

dawg … dog

ut … it

reglar … regular

offen … often

loike … like

ovva … of a

agin … again

noww … now

kneow … know

uz … is

troiyun … trying

eowners … owners

sumfun … something

wha'dut … what it

ivver … ever

annut … and it

thull … there'll

"Eeya Reg, hev yew ivver newtussed when yew lay in'ya bed ut noight yew can hear a dawg a barkun in the distance, annut seems tew bark inna reglar sequence. More offen an' not thay bark loike this:

Bark…   Bark, bark....   Bark, bark, bark!

Then thull be a bit ovva pause an' then ut'll dew ut all over agin.

Noww wha' yew don' knew uz, these dawgs are troiyun t'tell their eowners sumfun, … Dew yew wanna knew wha'dut uz?

Uts simple, uts:

" Oi …   Oi, yew …   let me in!"

45

arf … half

'ate … hate

blews … blows

coed … cold

floiy … fly

troiyun … trying

ruud … road (pronounced as in stood, hood)

gort … got

cowt … coat

trewsers … trousers   fewd … food

lorst … lost

gorn … gone

brook … broke

droiy … dry   floiy … fly   oiyes … eyes

noww … now

dussen … do not   ringum … phone them

Oi don't arf 'ate the wind …
   cuz ut blews me hair about,
an' when uts really icy coed
   the drips floiy orf me snout.

Sometoimes ut makes me stagger
   troiyin' t'git up the ruud,
'specially if oi gort the wrong cowt on
   an' the wind gits in me hood.

Me trewsers have flapped loike crazy,
   sew much they've stung me legs,
an' once oi lorst me shoppun bag
   an' gorn an' brook me eggs.

Then when uts droiy the dust can floiy
   intew ya oiyes fer sure,
an' when yew,ve managed tew clear 'em out,
   the wind blews in some more.

Noww oi dussen bother,
   oi'll stay in if oi can,
if oi need some fewd oi'll ringum up
   an' thay can bring ut in a van!

hay … have

y'gottum … you got them   yit … yet

hoe … no

corda … cor! the

welloos … well who's

'en … then

iron-o … I don't know

g'nah … going to

naow … no

hewp … hope

couz … because

om … I'm

shoulda … should have

heddum … had them

yistdee … yesterday

"… hay y'gottum yit?"

"Hoe … corda hell boiy oi int gottum!"

"Welloos gottum 'en?"

"Iron-o … oh, wait aminut he wer g'nah gettum … Oi BRIAN! … hay y'got 'em hooja maflips yit?"

"Naow, not yit!"

"Well gew gettum 'en."

" He's new g'nah gew gettum,roight bor!"

"Oi hewp sew, couz om in trouble if oi int gottum t'day … shoulda heddum yistdee!"

"Yew should be alroight, couz come t'morra t'day will be yistdee!"

alorng … along

earra … here a

hew … how

moiy … my

loine … line

bitta … bit of

hut … hurt

jus'wanna … just want to

fer … for

g'nah … going to

y'ron … you on

balonginna … belong in the

warta … water

spuus … suppose (as in 'puss' – cat)

whew … who   oime … I'm

couz … because

Alorng the river oi loike tew gew a fishun,

but oi spend tew much toime
                    sittin' earra wishun.

Come on yew fish,
            hew lorng av oi gotta wait,

on the end ov me loine, airs a lovely
                            bitta bait.

Oi int g'nah hut ya, oi jus'wanna catch
                        ya fer fun,

then oi'll let y'ron gew agin where yew
                        balonginna sun.

Thay say fish int sew clever, but whew
                        are thay t'say,

couz oi cant seem t'catch ya, and oi've
                    sat 'ere arf a day!

If oi can see ya inna warta, oi spuus yew
                        can see me tew,

oime not sure whews the smarter, but oi
                think ut looks loike yew!

marnt … must not

int … am not

g'noo … going to

wernt … was not

heddunt … had not

abowdut … about it

'en … then

dint … didn't

wellus … well it's

jussus … just as

"…Yew marnt!"

"Oi int!"

"Yew wer g'noo!"

"Oi wernt!"

"Yew heddunt better!"

"Oi thort abowdut!"

"Well there yew are 'en!"

"But oi dint, did oi!"

"Wellus jussus well 'en!"

moight … might

floiy … fly   troiy … try

ut … it

grut … great

moiy … my   woifes … wifes

"Eeya, Reg …
        Oi wonder hew many squirrels are afraid
 ov hoights?"

Pigs moight floiy,

oi saw one troiy

ut wer up an apple tree.

Ut took a grut leap

an' fell inna heap,

noww uts wrapped up

in moiy woifes best paysteree!

mornun … morning

gorn … going

int … am not

bin … been

oivor … either

youra … you're a

dorn … doing

omma … I am a

hewle … hole

ev ya … have you

hev … have

foind … find

" mornun George, where ya gorn tew 'en?"

"Oi int gorn anywhere!"

"Oh … Where ya bin 'en?"

"Oi int bin anywhere oivor!"

"Tha' don't make alotta sense bor, don't yew knaow what youra dorn?"

"Omma lookun!"

"Lookun fer what?"

"Oi gotta hewle in me pocket! …"

"Oooh … Lorst some money ev ya … hew much hev ya lorst 'en?"

"Oi dunno, but oi will when oi foind ut!"

The sun is warm
    upon me back,

as oi walk along
    this ancient track,

with hawthorn flowers
    sew whoite 'nd broight,

'nd the smell sew sweet …

Oo'argh,
    oive got kippers tonoight!

"Eeya Reg …

Hev yew newtussed tha' there be floies

about inna winter toime naow …

mus'be all t'dew with this modern
ticknology …

they gotta be wearin' thermal underwear
or sumfun!"

trewsers … trousers

innut … in it

hed … had

moiy … my

ov 'em … of them

couz … because

threwn … thrown

artawuuds … afterwards

unnerneath … underneath

Tha' bloomin' ole bramble is prickly ole stuff,
 oive caught me trewsers innut enough.

Them hooks 'n' barbs are as sharp as can be
an' oive hed moiy fair share ov 'em stuck in me.

But all in all, oi shouldn't grumble,
couz oi loike 'em berries when threwn inna
                                    crumble.

Custard on top an' sew sweet unnerneath,
then artawuuds yew'll be pickun the pips from
                                    y'teeth!

nixt … next

arewnd … around   sewnd … sound

air-ra … there a   tewtlly … totally

oiyes … eyes   woide … wide

layun … laying   troiyun … trying

couz … because   roull … roll

arta … after   t'ya … to your

uzza … is a   toiyred … tired

bin … been

agin … again

Are you remembering the silent 'T's?

Dew yew hev troubles in ya bed
that cause yew nixt mornun tew feel arf dead,
wivva sleepless noight ov tossin' arewnd,
whoile ya partner lays air-ra sleepun tewtlly sewnd.

Roull on t'ya left, roull on t'ya roight,
whoiy cant oi git tew sleep tonoight.
Moiy oiyes int toiyred, oi feel woide awake,
whatsa point ov layun 'ere fer geudness sake.

Oi gave up troiyun tew count some sheep
couz arta foive thewsand oi jus' wanted tew weep.
Peepun ut the clock uzza bad thing t'dew,
fer what seems loike ten minutes uts probably bin tew.

Then the missus pulls the quilt uncoverun me arm,
then oi wrench ut roight back agin 'nd troiy t'keep calm.
Oi marnt lewse me temper, uts frustratun fer sure,
'specially when she starts snorun a lot louda than afore.

Yew'll git tew the point when yew dew fall asleep
an' ut int long arta yew'll start hearun that bleep.
Yew switch orff the alarm an' ya drift orff agin',
nixt toime yew wake up, yew've got work…
start panickin'!

ee … he

omma … I'm a

telluts … tell it's

wha'ee … what he

wassat … whats that

difrunt … different

wivvut … with it

hew … who

dornt … don't

"… ee is!"

"Ee innnt!"

"Ee is omma tellun'ya!"

"Ca'mon George, ut cant be!"

"Ut is, oi can telluts Jorhnee Depp couz oi naow wha'ee dew in 'em films."

"Wassat 'en?"

Well,ee always make 'imself look difrunt an' use difrunt voices t'gew wivvut."

"Bit loike yew arta afew drinks 'en … sew ow can yew telluts really 'im 'en?"

"Couz oime loike that detectuv Hercules Pie-rot, oi gotta an oiye fer spottun these things!"

"Hew … hewda hells Hercules Pie-rot?"

"Cor da hell boiy, oi moight as well be talkun tew meself … dornt yew watch the telly?"

"Cors oi dew … but yew gotta remember moiy tellies a difrunt make t'yours!"

o'woine … of wine

foine … fine

ov … of

hid … head

oive … I have

nixt … next

Oi dew loike a drop ov woine,

jus' a little will dew me foine.

A drop ov red, a drop ov whoite

can make me hid gew funny an' loight.

Hev tew much as oive done afore,

will nixt mornun give me a hid sew sore.

'Everythun in moderation' uz wha' thay say…

Sew oive harved me intake…

… tew jus' a bottle a day!

blewk …bloke (man)

dorn'at … doing that

dewwut … do it

noice … nice

slew … slow   foyah … for you

hay … have

naow … now

dornt … don't   whin … when

sumfun … something

shoont … shouldn't

aboutut … about it

dint … didn't

smoiled … smiled

axunt …accent

'as 'im … that's him

whews … who's

"…Sew oi said tew this posh blewk, 'Yew marnt be a dorn'at boiy!' an' wivva farnee look ee said in his posh voice, 'I beg your pardon?' … Oi said agin, 'Yew marnt dewwut!'

'Sorry old chap, I don't follow, it's your accent, I'm not familiar with marnt!' ee said. Oi said, 'Roight boiy, oi'll say ut noice un slew foyah … Yeww muust norrt dewwut … marnt! … Hay yew gort tha' naow!'

'Yes' ee said, 'I think so, but I wasn't going to light up yet!'

'Well 'as alroight 'en, but tha' dornt arf roile me up whin oi see people dew sumfun tha' knew thar shoont thus all!' oi said.

"Ee wer alroight aboutut an' dint say n'more, jus' smoiled … blinkun cheek sayun oi gort a an axunt … 'as 'im whews gort an axunt!"

ghewsts … ghosts

tind … tend

sewnd … sound

ovva … of a

leggut … (run off)

instid … instead

listnun … listening

cun … can

poipes … pipes   oiyes … eyes

tewwum … to them

moind … mind

aloined … lined   attut … at it

phewto …photo

knaow … know

newtussed …noticed   naow … no

sin … seen   bin … been

Oi don' really believe in ghewsts
　　　　thar jus' int naow such thing,
people tind tew froightun th'mselves
　　　　an' dew tew much imaginin'.

The sewnd ovva creak or ov
　　　　footsteps onna floor,
an' these silly sods gew an' leggut
　　　　instid ov listnun some more.

Noises cun come about in poipes an' wood,
　　　　jus' from the hot or the cold,
but naow matter what yew say tewwum
　　　　they don' really want t'be told.

Yer oiyes cun play tricks'
　　　　an' yer moind can tew,
sew oive gorta little ixperiment
　　　　aloined up fer yew.

Loork atta phewto
　　　　ov someone yew knaow,
an' stare attut constantly
　　　　fer a minute or sew.

Then quickly loork away
　　　　ut a clean empty space,
blink loike the clappers
　　　　an' yew should see a face.

Thas all people have newtussed an' sin,
Thar int bin naow ghewsts, jus' some story tellin'!

docta … doctor

n'newtuss … no notice

uz … is

compewters … computers

inuff … enough ixcersoise … excercise

lewsun … loosing tempa … temper

naow … no probblee … probably

omma … I am

larnun … learning

swallarin … swallowing

warta … water

Are you remembering those silent 'T's. War-ah.

poiynts … pints

"Me docta said oi gort tew cut dewn on me drinkun couz uts bad fer me."

"Wha', yew don' wanta take new newtuss ov 'im, couz jus' about everythuns bad fer ya t'day…

suckun fags uz bad fer ya,
eatun tew much uz bad fer ya,
watchun tew much telly uz bad fer ya,
loorkun at 'em compewters uz bad fer ya,
workun lorng hours uz bad fer ya,
droivun on 'em busy ruuds uz bad fer ya,
nort gittun inuff sleep uz bad fer ya,
nort gittun inuff ixcersoise uz bad fer ya,
joggun uz bad fer ya,
lewsun ya tempa uz bad fer ya…

oi reckun tew much hews ya father uz probblee bad fer ya tew…even breathun moight be…sew oi don' take n'newtuss ov ut all…

sew hew much hev ya bin a drinkun 'en, foive, six, siven points a noight?"

"Naow, ut int nothin' tew dew wiv beer…omma larnun tew swim, an' oi keep swallarin the warta!"

73

thus … this

corf's … cough's

huttun … hurting

hid … head

makun … making

arta … after

toime … time

onnuts … on it's

wust … worst

'tillut … until it

almust … almost

wennuts … when it's

gorn … gone

bendun … bending

Thus blarsted corf's
        gittun on me wick,
uts huttun me hid
        makun ut feel roight thick.

Seems tew gew on an' on
        day arta day,
 'bout toime ut cleared up
        an' went onnuts way.

Noight toimes the wust
        as oi lay in me bed,
when tha' tickle starts up
        th' feels loike a thread.

Ut itches an' tickles
        'tillut droives me quoit mad,
almost corf up me lungs
        an' make me feel roight bad.

Oi'll be glad wennuts gorn
        ut'll be sucha relief,
couz oime fed up bendun dewn
        tew retrieve me false teeth.

boiy ... by

squit ... sh!t

dint ... didn't

oiye ... eye

wuss ... worse

tuufbrush ... toothbrush

arf ... half

grew ... grow

dunnut ... don't it

y'roiyes ... your eyes   y'cun ... you can

agotta ... have got to   agrewwun ... a growing

betterun ... better than   fr'm ... from

moine ... mine   'ere ... here

A bird flew boiy
an' squit in me oiye,
cor, ut dint arf sting.

Oi made ut wuss
when oi used a tuufbrush
tew clean out the stingy thing.

*   *   *   *   *   *

"Tha' ole grass don' arf grew dunnut?"

"Cor, da hell bor, y'roiyes agotta be betterun moine if y'cun see 'at agrewwun fr'm 'ere!"

uvver … other

avvun … having

lewda … load of

wuds … words

wuz … was

nivver … never

moind … mind

dint … didn't

wha'y'mint … what you meant

oicun … I can

w'later … well later

wairzat … where's that

inny … any

wherrit … was it

'ump … hump (got annoyed)

oonly … only

wernut … wasn't it

huum … home

troiyun … trying

"Ole Jorhn made me laugh the uvver day, he wer avvun a roight lewda trouble gittun 'is wuds out…ee said "…thar wuz a puud widgeon in me gardun an' ut…"
"Oi said, 'wha', a puud widgeon, yew said puud widgeon Jorhn?'
'Naow oi dint!'
''fraid yew did, Jorhn!'
'Oi dint, oi said wuud pigeon!'
'Nivver moind oi knew wha' y'mint!'
'Oi dint say puud widgeon, oi now wha' oi said!'
'Alroight, alroight, nivver moind.' "Oi said…

Well… ee 'ad the roight 'ump wiv me arta tha' oicun tell ya…w'later on ,ee wer tellun me ee wer at 'is woifes sister's place ut Ringsfield. Oi said 'wairzat 'en?' an' ee said, 'Uts near Becky an' Bungles…'
"Oi said" 'Whew d'hell is Becky an' bungles, oi don' knew inny Becky an' Bungles?'
"Well, 'at wherrit wernut , ee gort in sucha 'ump oi hed t'gew huum…
Ee wer oonly troiyun t'say Beccles an' Bungay!"

79

oime … I am

hew … who

wiv … with

ov … of

mussun … mustn't

grut … great

rewst … roast

av …have

ifoiy … if I

ruum … room

tewwut … to it

Oime a man hew loikes 'is dinners
                    wiv plenty on the plate,

no worries ov wha' oi mussun eat,
                    no worries ov me weight.

Oi'll eat a grut rewst dinner
                    an' av seconds ifoiy can,

sew clear the ruum an' leave me tewwut,

couz there's a chance oi moight gew bang!

forrum … for them

onnabout … on about

attum … at them   clew … clue

donnay … don't they

orta … ought to

dewway … do they

spuus … suppose

moighta gorttun … might have got

sum'unair … something there

praps … perhaps

writ … written

lewpy … loopy

cluus … close

moighta … might have

doctus … doctors   wroitun's … writing has

innythun … anything

"Oi don' reckun 'as the roight name forrum!"

"Wha' yew onnabout noww,George?"

"Butterfloies."

"Butterfloies?"

"Ut carnt be roight, look attum!"

"Oi int gortta clew wha'yewwa gorn onnabout, George!"

"Oi werra thinkun about th'way thay werra flutterun… thay flutta donnay?"

"Well ats wha' thay normally dew!"

"Well oi reckun thay orta be called flutterfloies, don' make butter dew'ay?"

"Flutterfloies?…spuus yew moighta gorttun sum'unair."

"Praps uts t'dew wiv the way ut wer writ one toime,couz if someone hed writ a lewpy letta F tew cluus tew the letta L, ut moighta looked loike a letta B!"

"Possible oi spuus … 'specially if moiy doctus wroitun's gort innythun t'gew boiy!"

loorked … looked

mirra …mirror

dewsey … (dopey, stupid)

coont … couldn't

'andsum … handsome

wuz … was

twinty … twenty

ewnly … only

wanta … want to

crabby … (tired, worn, aged)

phewto … photo

innuts … in it's

Oi lorked in the mirra,
              wha' did oi see,
some dozey ole sod,
              ut coont be me.

Oi used t'be 'andsome,
              a looka wuz oi,
but oi wer then twinty
              an' ewnly a boiy.

Oi don' wanta loork
              at tha' crabby ole face,
oi'll sling tha' mirra

              an' put a phewto innuts place.

wunda … wonder

dureckon … do you reckon

whennay … when they

woont … wouldn't

dewwum … do them

geud … good

woodut … would it

ivver … ever

y'makun … you're making

wunderun … wondering

nivver moind … never mind

airs … there's

iffairs … if there's

air … there

"Eeya, Reg, oi wunda if bats are loike people?"

"Wha'ya mean?"

"Well dureckon thay gew deaf whennay git old…
ut woont dewwum alotta geud woodut!"

"Dew yew ivver wunda about y'self George?"

"Whoiy?"

"Couz y'makun me begin t'wunda!"

"Wha' yew a wunderun 'en?"

"Nivver moind…oh loork, airs a rabbut come out ov uts
'ole!"

One minute later.

"Eeya, Reg, oi wunda iffairs rabbuts out air thatta
Claustraphewbic?"

whin ... when

stoile ... stile

draws ... (trousers)

lewd ... loud

arewnd ... around

hedda ... had to

innyway ... anyway

tunned ... turned

onnis ... on his

oiken ... I can

dinnut ... didn't it

nuttun ... nothing

izzut ... is it

corse ... of course

snew ... snow

woont ... wouldn't

wintun ... went an

frit ... frightened

g'nah ... going to

newtussun ... noticing

ivryone ... everyone

ahoind ... behind

th'arse ... the backside

shut ... shirt

abowdut ... about it

hooly ... (really,extremely)

nivver ... never

ovva ... of a

yewd ... you'd

fust ... first

"...sew whin oi put me roight leg over the stoile, me draws wintun split roight uppa middle, ut wer tha' lewd ut frit ole Bill's cows.

Innyway, oi filt arewnd me hind quarters an' knew me jackut weren't g'nah coverut sew oi knew oi hedda be lucky t'get threw the village wivvout someone newtussun. Corse, oi wern't g'nah be tha' lucky couz ut seemed loike ivryone wer about – sods law, wernut!

Oi passed Mrs. Jamesun wiv naow trouble, then Arthur Tye, whin ole Jorhn tunned up ahoind me onnis boike an' roight out lewd ee gews;

'Eeya George, yew realoize yew gort th'arse outta ya trewsers, oiken see y'ole shut ahangun out?'

Corse 'at made a few loork arewnd dinnut!

'Whoiy don' ya make a public announcemunt abowdut!' Oi said.

Ee said; "At int nuttun t'worry about izzut! Must be hooly draughty rewnd ya nivver regions, oi'da thort!'

Oi said; 'Corse ut flippun is. If yew jumped out ovva plane inna snew storm wearun a kilt, yewd be feelun a draught rewnd ya nivver regions tew, woont ya?'

'Nort ifoiy come dewn hid fust oi woont!' ee say.

Food for thought.

Earlier I had mentioned how the accent can vary from one area to another and amazingly it can be within just a few miles distance to have an effect.

For example, some people in the Ipswich area may say 'owd' for old, but in Stowmarket which is not much more than 10 miles away, you hear people say 'ole', that's old with no letter 'd' at all – 'Tha' ole thing!' – Strange isn't it!

But just to get you thinking - and this is for all dialects and accents around the country - all have to merge very softly into the next – there's no getting away from it!

Imagine for a moment a giant map of East Anglia covered with a pool of water. If we throw an imaginary stone into the water, the ripples will stretch out in all directions quite strongly to start with and then slowly diminish. On the 5 mile mark it will have lost half of its strength. I believe this is the reaching distance of your very own, local accent.

To get a better picture of how our accent changes on this 5 mile mark, I'll now use something we can all relate to – a cheese and pickle sandwich.

If the Ipswich accent is slightly different to that of Hadleigh, the villages in between on the 5 mile mark will have a small flavouring of both accents within. If the Ipswich accent is a full cheese and pickle sandwich, half the pickle will have gone just 5 miles down the road. On reaching Hadleigh, that sandwich may consist of only bread and cheese. Another 5 miles further, and half the cheese will have gone, so by the time you reach Sudbury it would only consist of the bread and butter. So as you can see that by the time you reach Halstead in Essex the sandwich will be more or less non-existent. The full Suffolk accent will have gone.

The Essex accent has then started to take hold and gets stronger as you move further south.

As I said, it happens throughout the spread of the land and we're all pretty much unaware of it going on around us. I find it all rather fascinating.

Innyway, keep ya ole ear'oles owpen an' avva geud ole lissun out there. Uts noice tew hear folk talk!

Foind ut quick.

If by chance you took a liking to my pencil drawing of the talented Mr.Johnny Depp, I can have one printed for you on an A3 card (approx.16"x12") for just £5.00 including postage and protective packaging. Just write to me with your name, address with postcode and a cheque made out to Adrian Copping, and one will be on it's way to you a.s.a.p. Why not make it a gift!

66 Edgecomb Road,
Stowmarket,
Suffolk IP14 2DW.

Also available is my first book entitled 'Scrambled Guppy', Angler to Scrambler.
It contains 120 pages of stupidity and madness, as I fulfilled a dream to become a scrambles rider in the late 1970s.
Ideal for those with an interest in motorcycles or past experiences of scrambles meetings.
Only £5.00 inc. p&p from the same address above.